The Pitt: Inside TV's Boldest Medical Drama

An In-Depth Companion Guide to the Characters, Stories, and Cultural Impact of the Groundbreaking Series

DENA T. WARK

Contents

Chapter 1

Introduction to *The Pitt*

A New Medical Drama for a New Era

Television has always had a fascination with the hospital setting. From the frantic beeping of monitors to the charged silence before a surgeon makes a life-or-death call, the medical drama genre has provided some of the most gripping moments in TV history. But in January 2025, a new show burst onto the scene with an ambition that went beyond the usual formula. That show is *The Pitt*.

Unlike the standard episodic medical dramas of the past, *The Pitt* dares to slow time down. It doesn't rush through multiple cases across a single episode. Instead, it takes one single shift in the emergency room—fifteen hours in total—and spreads it across fifteen episodes. Each installment represents one hour of a harrowing, pressure-packed day inside Pittsburgh Trauma

Medical Center's emergency department, a hospital so intense that staff have nicknamed it "the Pitt."

This fresh approach immediately marked it as something more than just another medical series. It positioned *The Pitt* as a bold experiment in immersive storytelling, one that mirrors the chaos and relentlessness of real-life medicine. Viewers are not just watching a hospital show; they are living through the shift alongside the characters, breath by breath, crisis by crisis.

The Creative Minds Behind the Series

At the heart of *The Pitt* lies a team of television veterans who understand both the art of drama and the nuances of the medical field. The show's creator, R. Scott Gemmill, is no stranger to high-stakes storytelling, having worked extensively on shows like *NCIS: Los Angeles* and *ER*. His vision for *The Pitt* was to create something grounded, raw, and emotionally truthful—a show that strips away glossy portrayals of hospital life and digs deep into the reality of trauma care.

Backing him is executive producer John Wells, a name that carries enormous weight in television. Wells was instrumental in the success of *ER*, widely considered the gold standard of medical dramas. His presence on *The Pitt* not only adds credibility but also reassures audiences that the emotional authenticity and layered storytelling that defined *ER* are being channeled into this new project.

And then there is Noah Wyle, whose involvement ties the show directly to the legacy of *ER*. Wyle, who played Dr. John Carter for years, returns here not as a young resident but as a seasoned actor carrying the emotional gravity of decades spent in and around fictional hospitals. His performance is central to why fans and critics alike are calling *The Pitt* one of the most compelling dramas of the decade.

A Fresh Take on the Medical Genre

Medical dramas have traditionally followed a fairly predictable rhythm. Each episode introduces several cases, interspersed with glimpses of doctors' personal lives, all tied together neatly within forty-five minutes. It's a formula that has worked for decades. But *The Pitt* breaks away from that pattern.

By stretching one shift over fifteen episodes, the show creates a relentless sense of time pressure. Doctors don't get to wrap up one case before moving to the next; instead, problems overlap, pile up, and linger. A critical patient might be rushed in during Episode 2, and viewers are still seeing the consequences of that same case in Episode 7. This format mirrors reality more closely, because in actual hospitals, crises don't neatly resolve on schedule.

What's more, the show does not shy away from silence, fatigue, or the messy, uncertain nature of medicine. Sometimes, a diagnosis isn't clear. Sometimes, a doctor makes the wrong call. And sometimes, despite every heroic effort, the patient doesn't make it. These moments add emotional weight, grounding the show in truths that resonate with healthcare workers worldwide.

Realism That Hits Home

One of the reasons *The Pitt* stands out is its unwavering commitment to realism. Every detail—from the pacing of medical procedures to the frantic coordination between nurses, residents, and attending physicians—feels meticulously researched. Medical consultants were heavily involved in production to ensure accuracy, and it shows.

Doctors and nurses who have watched the show have praised its ability to capture both the technical aspects of trauma care and the emotional strain of working in emergency medicine. Unlike shows that prioritize flashy surgeries or over-the-top melodrama, *The Pitt* is unafraid to depict the quieter, heavier toll of exhaustion, moral injury, and compassion fatigue. In doing so, it has won admiration not just from entertainment critics but also from those on the frontlines of healthcare.

The Global Context of *The Pitt*

While set in Pittsburgh, the themes explored in *The Pitt* are universal. Every country has its own version of underfunded hospitals, overworked doctors, and health systems stretched to their breaking points. In the aftermath of the COVID-19 pandemic, these issues are not only relevant—they are painfully familiar.

International audiences connect to the sense of burnout, the resilience of medical workers, and the haunting reality of trauma medicine. Whether viewers are in Lagos, London, or Los Angeles, the stress of emergency care is instantly recognizable. This global relatability has fueled its rising popularity, making *The Pitt* not just an American drama but an international talking point.

The Critical Reception

From the moment it premiered, *The Pitt* drew widespread attention. Critics praised it for its bold narrative structure, its unflinching realism, and the powerhouse performances of its cast. Within weeks of airing, it earned a 95% approval rating on major review aggregators, with many reviewers calling it a worthy successor to *ER*.

The industry also took notice. The series secured thirteen Emmy nominations in its debut season, winning multiple awards including Outstanding Drama Series. The recognition cemented its place as not just a popular show but a groundbreaking entry into television history.

A New Standard in Television Storytelling

Perhaps what makes *The Pitt* most compelling is the way it redefines what television can be. Instead of delivering quick resolutions and predictable arcs, it asks audiences to commit— to sit in the tension, to feel the fatigue of long shifts, to wrestle with the uncertainty of medicine. This is storytelling that trusts its viewers, treating them not as passive consumers but as participants in a shared experience.

The Pitt doesn't simply entertain. It challenges. It asks hard questions about the state of healthcare, about the cost of compassion, and about the humanity of those working under impossible conditions. In doing so, it has raised the bar not just for medical dramas but for modern television as a whole.

Chapter 2

The Birth of *The Pitt*

A Vision Sparked by a Changing World

The origins of *The Pitt* trace back to a simple yet powerful idea: what if a medical drama could slow time down and show audiences the unfiltered, exhausting pace of real-life emergency medicine? R. Scott Gemmill, the creator, wanted to move away from the neat packaging of conventional television storytelling and lean into something messier, more relentless, and far more human.

Gemmill had spent years building his reputation in television, contributing to projects that thrived on intensity and high stakes. But the seeds of *The Pitt* were planted after observing the shifting cultural landscape. The COVID-19 pandemic had forced the world to reckon with the realities of healthcare in ways it never had before. Suddenly, the heroism and burnout of medical workers were no longer abstract concepts; they were lived experiences, often witnessed on the evening news.

Gemmill saw an opportunity to translate those experiences into storytelling. His vision was not just to entertain but to illuminate—to pull audiences into the heart of trauma care in a way that was authentic and emotionally gripping. For him, *The Pitt* was not simply another hospital drama but a platform to reflect the courage and fragility of the human condition.

The Role of R. Scott Gemmill

Gemmill's creative philosophy has always leaned toward high realism. In *The Pitt*, he applied that philosophy with remarkable focus. He designed the show's structure around a single 15-hour shift in an emergency room, allowing for an unusual level of continuity. Instead of tidily resolving storylines in forty-five minutes, Gemmill wanted to explore the lingering consequences of trauma, mistakes, and tough choices.

What made Gemmill the perfect figure to spearhead this project was his background. His work on *ER* gave him firsthand exposure to how medical storytelling could grip an audience while still respecting medical science. With *The Pitt*, however, he aimed to go further. Where *ER* captured the sweep of hospital life over years, *The Pitt* would capture the urgency of a single day, minute by minute. It was both an artistic risk and a bold statement about the possibilities of television drama.

John Wells and the Power of Legacy

If Gemmill was the architect, John Wells was the cornerstone that anchored the project. Wells is a name synonymous with quality in American television. His fingerprints are all over *ER*, a series that not only broke ratings records but also reshaped how audiences viewed the medical drama genre.

When Wells came aboard *The Pitt*, it was more than a professional collaboration; it was a passing of the torch. His presence gave the new series legitimacy and continuity with television history. Wells understood the pressures and expectations of crafting medical drama at the highest level, and his involvement reassured both the creative team and the network that *The Pitt* would be built on firm foundations.

Wells's influence extended beyond production logistics. His knack for balancing character-driven storytelling with large ensemble casts is evident throughout the show. Under his guidance, the series avoided becoming purely procedural or purely melodramatic. Instead, it found a space in between— where the medical emergencies mattered as much as the inner lives of those working through them.

The Casting of Noah Wyle

One of the most talked-about decisions in the making of *The Pitt* was the casting of Noah Wyle. To fans of medical dramas, Wyle is almost inseparable from his iconic role as Dr. John Carter on *ER*. Bringing him into *The Pitt* was both a nostalgic callback and a strategic choice.

Wyle's casting was not simply a matter of star power. His decades of experience in medical drama gave him an instinctive understanding of the rhythms, jargon, and emotional stakes of hospital life. More importantly, Wyle brought gravitas. He was no longer the wide-eyed young doctor of the nineties; he was a seasoned performer capable of portraying layered emotions, moral conflict, and the quiet resilience of a veteran physician.

For audiences, his presence served as a bridge. Longtime fans of *ER* could see in Wyle a continuity of tradition, while new viewers discovered an actor capable of anchoring a complex and modern drama. His role in *The Pitt* reminded everyone that medical dramas are not only about the emergencies—they are also about the people who endure them.

Building the Connection to *ER*

It is impossible to discuss *The Pitt* without acknowledging its connection to *ER*. The parallels are intentional and, in many ways, unavoidable. Both shows deal with the chaos of emergency medicine, the strain on staff, and the moral dilemmas faced daily. Both rely on ensemble casts where every character matters, from attending physicians to interns and nurses.

Yet, while *ER* established the framework, *The Pitt* expanded it into new territory. Where *ER* spanned years of hospital life, *The Pitt* compresses time, creating a suffocating, almost claustrophobic intensity. This structure forces the audience to sit with unresolved tension, much like real doctors must do when answers are not immediate.

The legacy of *ER* also provided both a challenge and an advantage. On the one hand, *The Pitt* risked being labeled a remake or imitation. On the other, it benefited from the institutional memory of a show that once dominated television. By embracing familiar creative hands like Wells and Wyle while carving out its own narrative identity, *The Pitt* managed to honor its predecessor without being overshadowed by it.

The Creative Risks Involved

Bringing *The Pitt* to life was not without challenges. Networks and producers are often wary of unconventional formats, and the idea of devoting an entire season to one shift might have seemed risky. Would audiences have the patience for such sustained tension? Would the slower burn appeal in a world accustomed to quick resolutions and binge-worthy twists?

Gemmill and his team believed the risk was worth taking. They argued that television was evolving, and viewers were ready for deeper immersion and more daring formats. The gamble paid off. Instead of alienating audiences, the structure became one of the show's greatest strengths. It differentiated *The Pitt* in a crowded market and sparked critical discussions about the future of serialized storytelling.

The Collaboration of Industry Veterans

Beyond Gemmill, Wells, and Wyle, the birth of *The Pitt* was marked by the involvement of numerous seasoned professionals in television writing, directing, and production design. Many of them had prior experience with medical dramas, bringing with them both technical expertise and an understanding of audience expectations.

The set design reflected this professionalism. The hospital environment was recreated with meticulous detail, from the placement of medical instruments to the buzz of staff moving through cramped corridors. This attention to realism made the emergency room feel less like a set and more like a living, breathing space—a crucial element for a show that asks viewers to spend fifteen straight hours in that environment.

A Timely Arrival

The timing of *The Pitt's* debut in early 2025 could not have been more significant. The world was still dealing with the aftershocks of the pandemic, healthcare debates were ongoing in many countries, and audiences were more aware than ever of the sacrifices made by medical workers. Against this backdrop, *The Pitt* was not just another show—it was a cultural moment.

Its creation and birth reflected the intersection of history, necessity, and artistry. The show gave viewers not only entertainment but also a mirror to see the struggles of frontline workers in a format that was both respectful and riveting.

Chapter 3

Plot Structure and Storytelling Approach

Breaking the Traditional Mold

One of the most striking features of *The Pitt* is its refusal to follow the usual rhythm of television storytelling. For decades, medical dramas have thrived on episodic arcs. A patient arrives, doctors scramble to save them, and within forty-five minutes a resolution is neatly tied up. Audiences have been conditioned to expect closure, whether in triumph, tragedy, or bittersweet compromise.

The Pitt deliberately turns this formula inside out. Instead of treating each episode as a self-contained story, it stretches a single emergency room shift over the entire season. Fifteen hours. Fifteen episodes. Each installment moves the clock forward by only one hour, and in that short window, viewers are plunged into the chaos of trauma medicine without fast-forwarding to easy answers.

This structure instantly creates a different emotional texture. The show resists the temptation to rush, forcing audiences to sit in the intensity of unfolding crises. The result is a deeply immersive experience that feels more like living through the shift alongside the doctors than watching a scripted drama.

The Power of Real-Time Storytelling

Real-time storytelling is not entirely new to television, but it is rare and difficult to sustain. The series *24* popularized the idea by compressing a day into twenty-four episodes, but that was set in the adrenaline-fueled world of counterterrorism. *The Pitt* takes this principle into the hospital, where the stakes are no less urgent but the crises are human rather than geopolitical.

The real-time format gives weight to every decision. A doctor doesn't just declare a treatment and move on. Instead, viewers see the slow, agonizing minutes as a procedure unfolds, the way a patient's condition can change second by second, or the way exhaustion sets into the staff as the hours grind on. This pacing builds suspense not through explosions or gunfights, but through something far more relatable: the fragile boundary between life and death.

Layering of Story Arcs

What makes the format especially effective is how it allows multiple storylines to overlap and interlock. In traditional shows, a patient's case might begin and end in a single episode, perhaps resurfacing later in a "special" arc. In *The Pitt*, cases stretch across multiple hours. A trauma patient who arrives in Episode 2 might still be fighting for their life in Episode 6. A seemingly minor injury may evolve into a major complication by Episode 9.

Meanwhile, the doctors' own stories unfold in parallel, shaped by the same passage of time. Fatigue grows, tempers flare, and mistakes happen. By keeping every thread bound to the same relentless clock, the show creates an interconnected web where no moment is wasted and no storyline feels disposable.

Building Unrelenting Tension

The clock is not just a structural device; it is a character in its own right. Every episode begins with the sense that another hour has passed, another chance has been lost, or another challenge is about to crash through the ER doors. This ticking pressure is ever-present, heightening urgency even in quieter scenes.

Unlike conventional dramas that ebb and flow with predictable peaks and valleys, *The Pitt* operates on sustained intensity. Even when the pace slows, the sense of looming crisis never disappears. A lull in one patient's case might be shattered by the arrival of a multi-casualty accident, or a routine procedure might spiral into a catastrophe. Because the show refuses to wrap things up neatly, viewers are left in a state of constant alertness, mirroring the state of the characters themselves.

Immersion Through Authenticity

Another key advantage of this structure is immersion. By refusing to skip ahead, *The Pitt* demands that the audience experience time as the doctors do. When they wait for test results, so do we. When they scramble to resuscitate a crashing patient, we feel the seconds stretching unbearably.

This immersion gives the show its emotional punch. Viewers are not simply observers; they are participants. They share the exhaustion when the clock ticks past the tenth hour. They feel the dread when another emergency case arrives just as the staff think they might have a moment to breathe. In many ways, the real-time approach transforms passive watching into active endurance, a rare feat in television drama.

Humanizing the Chaos

The storytelling approach also humanizes the often-abstract concept of medical drama. Instead of focusing solely on grand moments of triumph or loss, *The Pitt* lingers on the smaller, more human details. A nurse stealing a quick bite of food before the next trauma call. A doctor's hands trembling from fatigue after hours of surgery. A brief, quiet exchange between staff in the hallway that reveals more about their inner lives than any monologue could.

These moments are only possible because the structure allows time to breathe. By devoting entire episodes to single hours, the show has space to explore not just what happens in the ER, but how it feels to live through it. This attention to detail deepens the emotional connection between characters and viewers, making every storyline feel earned.

Complexity Without Confusion

At first glance, one might assume that such a structure would lead to confusion or drag. But *The Pitt* carefully balances complexity with clarity. Each hour is tightly focused, with cases introduced and revisited in ways that build coherence rather than clutter. The writers avoid overwhelming the audience by weaving stories that are emotionally distinct even when they unfold simultaneously.

This balance keeps the show compelling for both seasoned fans of medical dramas and newcomers who might otherwise be intimidated by too much jargon or technical detail. The format invites audiences to follow along step by step, making them feel like insiders rather than outsiders.

The Psychological Toll of the Format

The real-time approach doesn't only intensify the drama; it also mirrors the psychological toll on the characters. Doctors and nurses don't have the luxury of skipping to the end of a shift. They feel every grueling hour. They carry the weight of unresolved cases, personal struggles, and lingering doubts. By showing each hour in detail, the series highlights the cumulative strain of working in emergency medicine.

This design also deepens character arcs. Instead of compressing emotional growth into sudden leaps, the show allows small, incremental changes to accumulate. A resident's confidence might erode little by little over hours of pressure. A seasoned physician's calm exterior might crack only after ten hours of nonstop crisis. These subtle shifts would be lost in a faster-paced format, but here they are given space to breathe.

Redefining Viewer Expectations

Perhaps the most significant impact of *The Pitt's* structure is how it redefines what audiences expect from a medical drama.

By committing to this real-time format, the show invites viewers to trade quick gratification for deeper engagement. It rewards patience with richer emotional payoffs and forces audiences to confront the unpredictability of real medicine.

Instead of offering neatly wrapped resolutions, it leaves space for uncertainty. Instead of sweeping away the consequences of one case before moving to the next, it carries the weight of each decision forward. This approach may challenge viewers used to conventional pacing, but it also elevates the storytelling into something more profound.

Chapter 4

Character Analysis – The Heart of *The Pitt*

Characters as the Living Pulse of the Drama

At the foundation of *The Pitt* lies not just the stories of patients wheeled through its doors, but the very people who make up the trauma team. Without them, the series would be a sterile exercise in medical procedures. With them, it becomes a tapestry of resilience, conflict, and transformation. Each character is written with precision and purpose, embodying the contradictions of trauma medicine—strength and fragility, compassion and detachment, hope and despair. Their arcs give the show its humanity, keeping audiences emotionally invested long after the credits roll.

The Central Figure – The Steady Hand Amid the Storm

The lead presence in *The Pitt* anchors the chaos of the series. They are not portrayed as a flawless savior, but rather as someone holding steady in the eye of a storm. This character's strength lies in their calm authority and clinical brilliance. They navigate the trauma bay with poise, making decisions in seconds that carry lifelong consequences. Yet cracks appear in moments of vulnerability, when exhaustion threatens empathy or past scars resurface. Their arc demonstrates the delicate balance of leadership under fire: maintaining control while carrying the weight of every choice.

The Idealist – Guided by Conviction

Every team needs a soul, and in *The Pitt*, that role belongs to the idealist. This character is driven by conviction, seeing every patient as a story worth fighting for. They bring warmth into the room, often acting as the moral compass. Yet their flaw is their refusal to accept limits. In a setting where triage often means making impossible choices, this idealism breeds friction with colleagues who see medicine through a colder lens. The arc of this character highlights the painful lesson of compromise, showing how conviction can both inspire and endanger in equal measure.

The Realist – Grounded in Pragmatism

Counterbalancing the idealist is the realist. This character embodies clinical efficiency, able to act with precision even when others falter. Their blunt approach can appear abrasive, their decisions sometimes cold. But beneath the pragmatism is a deep understanding of survival—not just for patients, but for the team. Their flaw lies in the perception of being unfeeling, a trait that sparks frequent clashes with the idealist. Together, they embody the eternal struggle of trauma medicine: the pull between hope and harsh reality.

The Veteran Nurse – The Voice of Experience

While doctors often claim the spotlight, the trauma nurse in *The Pitt* is the glue holding the team together. This character represents years of lived experience on the floor. They move with instinct, often predicting outcomes before others see them. Their authority does not come from title, but from credibility built through survival. The weight of loss has left them with a hardened edge, sometimes slipping into cynicism. Yet this same depth of experience makes them indispensable. Their arc is one of rediscovering hope, even after years of carrying the scars of countless shifts.

The Ambitious Resident – Energy on the Edge

The ambitious resident injects *The Pitt* with youthful energy. They are eager, driven, and sometimes reckless. Their strength lies in enthusiasm, a willingness to push boundaries and absorb everything like a sponge. But their flaw is impatience.

Inexperience makes them stumble, and their confidence often runs ahead of their skill. Their journey is not about brilliance alone, but about learning humility—the painful realization that greatness requires time, discipline, and failure. Through them, audiences are reminded of the tension between ambition and wisdom in medicine.

The Conflicted Administrator – Balancing Books and Blood

Behind every trauma team lies a system, and in *The Pitt*, that system is embodied by the conflicted administrator. They are charged with keeping the hospital functioning, balancing resources, and negotiating with bureaucracy. Their strength lies in foresight and efficiency, yet their flaw is detachment. Patients can become numbers on a page, staff members reduced to scheduling units. Their arc is a study in compromise, showing the constant tug between the human urgency of the trauma bay and the institutional demands of survival.

The Troubled Doctor – Haunted but Brilliant

One of the show's most gripping characters is the troubled doctor—a healer whose brilliance is shadowed by personal demons. They might be haunted by addiction, fractured relationships, or their own past traumas. Their gift is undeniable; when others falter, they often find solutions that save lives. But their flaw is volatility, threatening both themselves and those around them. This character's arc becomes one of redemption, a portrait of fragility and strength intertwined. Audiences are drawn in by the paradox of someone capable of extraordinary healing while desperately in need of healing themselves.

The Ensemble as a Mirror of Trauma Medicine

What sets *The Pitt* apart is that no character exists in isolation. Their stories intersect like arteries in the living body of the show. The idealist pushes against the realist, the veteran nurse steadies the ambitious resident, the administrator collides with the troubled doctor. These dynamics reflect the reality of hospital life, where personalities and philosophies clash but must ultimately merge for the sake of survival. Together, the ensemble embodies the spectrum of trauma medicine: conviction, pragmatism, resilience, ambition, bureaucracy, and redemption.

Chapter 5

The Realism of Medicine on Screen

The Fine Line Between Drama and Authenticity

One of the most striking features of *The Pitt* is its commitment to capturing the world of trauma medicine with a sense of realism that feels immediate and unflinching. Audiences who tune into medical dramas are often divided into two groups: those who crave entertainment and those who seek authenticity. Balancing both is no easy task, but *The Pitt* threads this needle with precision. It is not just about fast-paced storytelling or emotional highs; it is about bringing viewers into an environment that mirrors the actual intensity of emergency medicine. The realism is not incidental—it is a deliberate choice, woven into the DNA of the show.

Medical Procedures as Storytelling Anchors

From the first episode, the series grounds itself in procedures that are both recognizable and technically correct. Intubations, chest compressions, sutures, and even complex interventions such as thoracotomies are presented with careful attention to detail. Instead of glossing over these moments with quick cuts or vague gestures, the show lingers on them just enough for the audience to feel their gravity. Every procedure becomes more than an act of medicine—it becomes a beat of the story.

By respecting the accuracy of these practices, *The Pitt* avoids reducing them to flashy spectacle. For example, chest compressions are not performed with perfect hair and dry brows; they are messy, exhausting, and relentless, reflecting the true demands placed on professionals during resuscitation. Even the smallest moments—like the way a nurse checks for IV access or how a resident calls out vitals—are handled with care, giving the audience a sense of immersion that is rarely achieved in television drama.

The Use of Medical Terminology

Language is a vital part of realism in a medical series, and *The Pitt* understands that correctly. The dialogue is laced with terminology, yet it never alienates the viewer. Doctors and nurses use acronyms like "BP" for blood pressure or "GCS" for Glasgow Coma Scale, just as they would in real life, but the context ensures clarity. For instance, when a physician orders "two units of O-neg stat," the urgency of the moment makes the meaning clear even to those without medical backgrounds.

This approach mirrors the environment of a real trauma bay, where communication must be both rapid and precise. The show avoids over-simplifying language, respecting viewers enough to let them absorb the jargon naturally. In fact, the authenticity of the terminology often becomes a subtle form of education, introducing audiences to the rhythms and shorthand of emergency medicine without ever feeling like a lecture.

Trauma Cases as Windows Into Reality

What separates *The Pitt* from other medical dramas is its bold approach to trauma cases. Instead of relying solely on exaggerated or improbable scenarios, the series roots itself in situations that reflect genuine emergencies: motor vehicle accidents, gunshot wounds, workplace injuries, cardiac arrests, and strokes. These are the bread-and-butter crises of trauma medicine, and their inclusion grounds the show in reality.

That said, the series does not shy away from complexity. It portrays multi-casualty incidents where resources are stretched thin, reflecting the way trauma teams often face overwhelming influxes of patients. The depiction of triage—the process of deciding who gets treated first when not everyone can be seen at once—adds layers of ethical and emotional tension. These cases are not just plot devices; they expose the audience to the reality that medicine is as much about difficult choices as it is about saving lives.

The Role of Healthcare Consultants

One reason the series feels so authentic is the heavy involvement of healthcare professionals behind the scenes. Producers and writers consulted with real doctors, trauma surgeons, and nurses to shape both the medical accuracy and the atmosphere of the show. Scripts were vetted for realism, ensuring that what appeared on screen reflected current medical practices rather than outdated techniques or television inventions.

This collaboration shows in the smallest details. The way a trauma surgeon dons gloves, the clipped pace of a code blue, or even the exhaustion etched into a nurse's face after hours on shift—all these nuances came from listening to professionals who live these realities daily. By bringing consultants into the creative process, *The Pitt* achieves a rare balance: it dramatizes without distorting, and it entertains without disrespecting the craft of medicine.

Capturing the Atmosphere of a Trauma Bay

Accuracy in medicine goes beyond procedures and terminology; it is also about capturing the emotional and sensory environment. *The Pitt* excels at this. The constant alarms of monitors, the hurried footsteps of staff, the hurried exchanges between physicians and nurses, and even the chaos of overlapping voices build an atmosphere that feels undeniably authentic.

Equally important is the depiction of fatigue and burnout. Characters show the toll of long shifts—slouched shoulders, weary eyes, and short tempers. This mirrors the reality of trauma medicine, where fifteen-hour shifts are not just storytelling devices but genuine experiences for professionals. The emotional realism of exhaustion, doubt, and even occasional detachment adds another layer of truth that resonates with viewers.

Balancing Accuracy with Narrative Flow

Of course, *The Pitt* remains a drama, and that means some liberties are taken. Medical procedures that might stretch over an hour in real life are condensed for pacing. Diagnoses sometimes arrive more quickly than they realistically would, and lab results return at television speed. But what is important is that these adjustments never break the illusion of authenticity. They serve the rhythm of storytelling while maintaining respect for medical reality.

In fact, the tension between accuracy and narrative is itself handled with elegance. When the show accelerates a process, it balances that by embedding subtle reminders of realism. For example, while test results may return sooner, the dialogue often acknowledges the waiting time that would normally occur. This careful blend ensures the drama never strays into pure fantasy.

The Human Cost of Accuracy

Perhaps the greatest achievement of *The Pitt*'s realism is not in the technical details but in its portrayal of the human cost of trauma medicine. The show captures the emotional aftermath for both patients and providers. Doctors do not walk away from a failed resuscitation untouched—they carry it with them, sometimes visibly, sometimes quietly. Nurses break down after particularly grueling cases, reflecting the emotional labor that is often invisible outside hospital walls.

The series also highlights the ripple effect of trauma cases. A car accident is not just a medical emergency; it is a family crisis. The realism comes not only in how the body is treated but also in how the emotional fallout is acknowledged. This layered approach to accuracy elevates the show beyond surface-level authenticity, creating a multidimensional portrait of medicine as lived experience.

The Global Lens of Medical Realism

What also makes *The Pitt* significant is its universal resonance. Trauma medicine is not confined to one city or one country—it is a global reality. By portraying authentic medical practices, the show speaks to healthcare workers worldwide who recognize the truths within the fiction. The cases and terminology may vary slightly by region, but the urgency, the exhaustion, and the humanity remain the same. This global recognition strengthens the show's impact, making it not just a drama but a mirror held up to the medical profession at large.

Chapter 6

Themes of Human Struggle and Resilience

The Constant Weight of Burnout

Behind the flashing lights of ambulances and the tense moments in emergency rooms, one of the most pervasive realities is burnout. It's not just exhaustion after a long day; it's the type of fatigue that settles deep into the mind and body. Television dramas often dramatize this by showing characters who push themselves through night shifts, skipping meals, or facing relentless trauma cases without pause. The truth is, in many healthcare systems across the globe, burnout is not a subplot but an everyday battle.

Medical professionals often work shifts that extend well beyond the traditional eight hours. In some countries, junior doctors may log more than 80 hours a week. This relentless pace can eat into sleep, family life, and mental health. On-screen, this struggle translates into storylines where characters begin to question their purpose, lash out at colleagues, or simply collapse from exhaustion. These portrayals mirror real reports of high turnover in emergency medicine, as well as the increased risks of depression and anxiety among healthcare workers.

For viewers, this theme of burnout doesn't just serve as dramatic tension—it reminds audiences that medicine is not fueled by heroics alone. It's carried on the backs of humans whose bodies and minds have limits, no matter how much passion drives them.

Grief as a Silent Companion

Grief is unavoidable in medicine. No matter how skilled a doctor or nurse is, no matter how advanced the technology, death is a frequent visitor in emergency care. What makes grief unique in this context is its double edge: professionals must grieve privately while still providing strength and comfort to others.

In medical dramas, we often see characters step into the break room to cry alone, or we watch them carry the burden of a lost patient for an entire season. In real life, grief takes many forms. A nurse may still remember the first child they couldn't save even decades later. A surgeon might replay a case in their mind, wondering if one different decision could have led to survival. These moments of loss build a heavy emotional archive that healthcare workers must carry, often without the space or tools to process it.

On-screen portrayals of grief allow audiences to witness this inner world, which is often invisible in reality. They reveal the humanity beneath the scrubs—the simple truth that saving lives does not shield one from mourning the lives that slip away.

Compassion at the Core

Despite burnout and grief, compassion remains the heartbeat of emergency medicine. It's what keeps professionals coming back shift after shift. Compassion shows up in the smallest gestures: holding a trembling hand, explaining a procedure in simple terms, or sitting silently with a family as bad news sinks in.

Medical dramas magnify these moments to remind viewers that healthcare is not only about science—it's about people. For audiences, these acts of compassion resonate deeply because they reflect universal human values. Whether in a trauma unit in Lagos, a clinic in Tokyo, or an ER in New York, kindness in the face of crisis transcends language and culture.

This compassion is also what distinguishes healthcare workers as more than technical experts. It highlights their role as guides through some of life's darkest hours. Television, by emphasizing this, bridges the gap between fiction and reality, helping viewers appreciate the emotional intelligence required in medicine as much as the technical skill.

Systemic Failures and Their Toll

One of the most sobering themes in emergency care, both on-screen and in real life, is systemic failure. This includes overcrowded hospitals, lack of equipment, underfunded departments, or bureaucratic delays that cost precious minutes. In dramas, these failures often provide high-stakes tension—doctors fighting over limited ventilators, paramedics improvising care because supplies run out, or administrators prioritizing budgets over patients.

In reality, these systemic cracks are not just plot devices; they define the daily experience of countless medical professionals. For example, in some parts of the world, emergency departments face wait times of over 12 hours. In low-resource regions, healthcare workers may operate without basic necessities like gloves or electricity during surgeries. Even in well-funded systems, insurance limitations and administrative red tape can delay critical treatment.

These failures leave professionals caught between their oath to heal and the limitations of the system they work in. For audiences, witnessing this struggle on television becomes an eye-opener, showing that medicine is not just a battle against disease but also against the machinery of flawed institutions.

Triumph Amid the Chaos

Perhaps the most compelling theme of all is resilience. Despite exhaustion, grief, and broken systems, stories of triumph keep both professionals and viewers invested. Resilience in emergency medicine is not about invulnerability—it's about the ability to bend without breaking.

On television, triumph often comes in the form of a miraculous save: the patient who survives against all odds, or the team that pulls together during a mass-casualty event. In real life, triumph is often quieter but no less significant. It might be the moment a doctor stabilizes a patient long enough for them to see their family again. It might be a nurse teaching a family how to care for a recovering loved one at home. These victories, large or small, fuel resilience.

What makes these triumphs so powerful is the contrast. They emerge from a backdrop of relentless struggle, making them feel earned and deeply moving. For viewers, these moments ignite hope—not only in medicine but in the human spirit's ability to endure and prevail.

The Global Dimension of Resilience

Though medical dramas are often set in specific countries, the themes of struggle and resilience are universal. A paramedic in Mumbai facing traffic delays, a rural doctor in Brazil improvising with limited resources, or a trauma surgeon in London dealing with overcrowding—all encounter the same emotional landscape of burnout, grief, compassion, systemic hurdles, and triumph.

Television brings these themes to an international stage, allowing audiences from different cultures to see their own healthcare challenges reflected in the struggles of fictional characters. This universality is what makes medical dramas such enduring and globally beloved stories.

Chapter 7

The Emotional Weight of Trauma

Trauma as More Than Physical Injury

When most people think of trauma, the first images that come to mind are wounds, broken bones, or dramatic resuscitations in the emergency room. But trauma does not stop at the body—it seeps into the mind, leaving invisible scars that can shape the lives of both patients and healthcare professionals. In medical dramas, this duality is often portrayed through parallel storylines: a patient learning to live after a devastating accident and a doctor grappling with the lingering effects of what they witnessed. This layered perspective reminds viewers that trauma is not a moment—it is an ongoing experience.

In real-world emergency medicine, practitioners understand that a car crash or a shooting does not end when the patient is stitched up or discharged. The psychological reverberations can last for months or years, manifesting as nightmares, panic attacks, or even a complete reshaping of a person's identity. Television series use these arcs to illuminate an essential truth: healing involves both the body and the spirit.

Patients and Post-Traumatic Stress

For patients, the aftermath of a traumatic incident often brings post-traumatic stress disorder (PTSD). This condition is more than a medical term—it is a daily disruption. A survivor of a near-fatal accident may flinch at the sound of tires screeching. A victim of violence may find it impossible to feel safe even in their own home. Medical dramas often dramatize this with scenes of patients waking up screaming, recoiling from routine procedures, or struggling with memory gaps.

While dramatized for television, these portrayals are rooted in verified medical knowledge. PTSD is a recognized mental health condition that can develop after a person experiences or witnesses a life-threatening event. Symptoms include hypervigilance, intrusive memories, avoidance of reminders, and emotional numbness. On-screen stories that show patients navigating these struggles help audiences appreciate that surviving a trauma is only the beginning of recovery.

Doctors Carrying Invisible Wounds

The other side of this equation is the toll trauma takes on the healers themselves. Emergency doctors, nurses, and paramedics are constantly exposed to human suffering at its most extreme. Unlike patients who may experience one catastrophic event, healthcare professionals may encounter dozens within a single week. This relentless exposure can lead to secondary trauma, moral injury, and even PTSD in the caregivers themselves.

Television often depicts this through storylines where a doctor relives a failed procedure in their dreams, avoids certain cases, or even begins to lose confidence in their own skills. These depictions are not exaggerations. Research shows that repeated exposure to traumatic events can leave healthcare professionals with emotional wounds as deep as those of the patients they treat. For some, the weight of these experiences leads to long-term psychological challenges, strained relationships, or the difficult decision to leave medicine altogether.

The Burden of Moral Injury

Beyond trauma itself lies another complex layer: moral injury. This occurs when professionals are forced into situations where they cannot act in alignment with their ethical values. In emergency care, moral injury may arise when limited resources mean choosing which patient gets the last ventilator, or when a doctor must follow an administrative decision that conflicts with their medical judgment.

On television, these moments are often used as climactic turning points in an episode. A surgeon may break down after losing a patient they could have saved if not for delays. A nurse may rage against a hospital system that prioritizes paperwork over treatment. For viewers, these moments highlight that the emotional toll of medicine is not just about witnessing trauma— it is also about being trapped in impossible choices.

In real life, moral injury has been increasingly recognized as a significant factor in healthcare burnout and depression. Unlike trauma, which is linked to external events, moral injury festers internally, eroding a professional's sense of identity and purpose. The inclusion of these themes in dramas helps bring visibility to the ethical weight carried by those in medicine.

Coping Mechanisms and Their Complexities

How do characters—and real professionals—cope with this emotional weight? Television shows often explore a wide range of coping strategies, some healthy, some destructive. A character may find solace in mentoring, turning their pain into teaching moments for younger doctors. Another might lean on camaraderie with colleagues, sharing dark humor or unspoken glances that convey mutual understanding.

Yet, the darker coping mechanisms are equally common: excessive drinking, isolation, or detachment from patients to create emotional distance. These portrayals, though sometimes dramatized, reflect the genuine complexity of coping in high-pressure environments. In reality, healthcare systems worldwide are beginning to integrate wellness programs, counseling services, and peer support groups, but stigma and time pressures often keep professionals from seeking help.

By showing both sides—the constructive and the destructive—television reminds audiences that resilience is not automatic. It is a fragile process that requires intentional support, both personal and institutional.

Trauma Rippling Through Relationships

The emotional weight of trauma rarely stays confined to the workplace. In both fiction and reality, it spills into relationships. Doctors may find themselves unable to communicate openly with spouses, weighed down by cases they cannot discuss due to privacy or pain. Patients may struggle to reconnect with families who do not understand the depth of their psychological scars.

Television often uses these relationship struggles to deepen character development. A surgeon may push away a partner out of fear of vulnerability, while a patient's family may fracture under the stress of caregiving. These storylines resonate because they reflect universal truths: trauma affects not only the person directly involved but also the network of people around them.

In real terms, this highlights the importance of family education and support systems. Counseling is often extended to family members, helping them understand what a loved one is going through. Without such support, trauma becomes a shared burden that erodes not just individuals but entire households.

When the Mask Cracks

Perhaps one of the most poignant elements of trauma on-screen is the moment when the mask cracks—the instant when a seemingly strong and invincible doctor or nurse reveals their vulnerability. This could be a breakdown in the locker room, a whispered confession to a colleague, or a sudden outburst during a tense case.

These moments resonate powerfully because they strip away the illusion of invulnerability. They remind viewers that healthcare professionals, despite their training and composure, are human beings carrying unimaginable emotional weight. For audiences, it can be both heartbreaking and affirming to see these characters falter, because it mirrors the reality that strength does not mean the absence of pain.

A Shared Human Experience

What makes the depiction of trauma so compelling in medical dramas is its universality. Whether you are a patient facing the aftermath of a car crash or a doctor haunted by a lost life, the emotional weight of trauma speaks to a shared human experience: the struggle to carry invisible burdens. These shows magnify what is often hidden, giving voice to pain that many endure in silence.

Through layered storytelling, they remind audiences that trauma is not confined to physical scars. It is written in sleepless nights, strained relationships, and ethical dilemmas that never leave the mind. And in doing so, they expand our understanding of what it truly means to live—and to heal—in the shadow of crisis.

Chapter 8

Cinematography and Direction

Crafting Atmosphere Through Visual Language

Every television series tells a story with words, but in *The Pitt*, the visuals speak just as powerfully as the dialogue. Cinematography and direction form the backbone of how audiences experience the raw urgency of trauma medicine. The way a camera lingers on a trembling hand, or the way lighting falls harshly over a crowded trauma bay, can heighten the emotional weight far beyond what is written on the page. This visual language allows viewers to feel as if they are inside the hospital itself—trapped in the noise, chaos, and fragile silences of life-and-death decisions.

The Visual Grammar of Chaos

One of the most distinctive qualities of *The Pitt* is how it uses camera movement to mirror the unpredictability of an emergency room. Handheld shots dominate the trauma scenes, creating a jittery, unstable frame that reflects the emotional and physical turbulence of medical crises. The shaky, restless motion pulls audiences into the intensity, making them feel the same unease and adrenaline rush that the doctors themselves are experiencing.

At the same time, directors know when to counter this chaos with stillness. A static shot may capture a patient's face just before surgery, or linger on a surgeon washing their hands in eerie silence. This visual pause contrasts sharply with the disorder around it, underscoring the gravity of a moment without the need for words.

Lighting as Emotional Undercurrent

Hospital lighting is notoriously sterile, yet *The Pitt* uses it with precision to tell its story. In bustling ER scenes, harsh fluorescent lights dominate, amplifying the cold efficiency of the environment. Yet during moments of vulnerability—such as a doctor confronting personal grief or a patient's family awaiting news—the lighting often shifts to softer, warmer tones.

This subtle contrast shapes the mood without breaking immersion.

Darkness, too, plays a role. Shadowed hallways, dimly lit offices, or flickers of light across monitors create an atmosphere of tension and uncertainty. Cinematographers employ these techniques not only to capture realism but also to suggest the mental weight carried by the characters. A single shadow on a physician's face can symbolize doubt, regret, or the crushing weight of responsibility.

Camera Angles and Perspective

In storytelling, where you place the camera determines where the audience's empathy lies. *The Pitt* uses a variety of perspectives to immerse viewers. Low-angle shots of doctors during critical procedures project authority and control, while high-angle shots of vulnerable patients on gurneys highlight fragility. The camera often shifts between these perspectives quickly, reminding the audience that power and vulnerability coexist constantly in trauma medicine.

One of the series' most striking choices is the frequent use of close-ups. A bead of sweat on a surgeon's temple, the twitch of a nurse's jaw as they hold back tears, or the rapid blinking of a patient waking from sedation—all are magnified to capture the inner battles that words cannot describe. These close-ups turn medical drama into deeply personal storytelling.

The Rhythm of Editing

Direction in *The Pitt* is as much about timing as it is about framing. The editing rhythm mirrors the fluctuating pace of hospital life. During code blue sequences, cuts are rapid, almost breathless, reflecting the urgency of trying to save a life in seconds. Conversely, post-trauma scenes slow down deliberately, allowing silence and longer takes to capture the emotional aftermath.

Cross-cutting is also used effectively, particularly when two medical crises unfold simultaneously. Viewers are forced to jump between rooms, feeling the overwhelming scale of emergencies in a trauma center. This narrative device emphasizes that while one doctor is fighting to save a patient from cardiac arrest, another across the hall is dealing with an equally urgent crisis.

Set Design and Immersive Realism

The set of *The Pitt* is more than a backdrop; it is an active participant in the story. Emergency departments are designed to feel claustrophobic—narrow hallways, overcrowded waiting areas, and trauma bays filled with equipment create a sense of suffocation. This intentional clutter reflects the reality of hospitals, where life-saving devices compete with limited space.

Attention to detail is evident in every corner. From surgical instruments laid out with precision to scuffed floors that hint at years of wear, the set design grounds the drama in authenticity. Even the background extras—nurses charting notes, janitors moving equipment, security guards calming relatives—add texture, ensuring that the hospital feels alive and fully inhabited.

Sound and Visual Synergy

While this chapter focuses on visuals, it is impossible to separate cinematography from sound. Direction often synchronizes camera movement with sound cues to amplify intensity. For instance, a rapid dolly-in on a patient coincides with the beeping of a monitor escalating. The audience doesn't just see the danger—they feel it rising in rhythm with the camera and audio combined.

Silence is equally powerful. Directors sometimes strip away sound entirely during pivotal moments—a failed resuscitation, a surgeon staring at their bloodied gloves—and allow the visual frame to carry the emotional load. The absence of noise becomes its own form of storytelling.

Movement Through Space

Hospital dramas often take place in confined environments, yet *The Pitt* uses creative blocking and tracking shots to make these spaces dynamic. Long takes following doctors through corridors connect multiple storylines seamlessly. A single tracking shot might move from a chaotic ER into a quiet waiting room, visually representing the dual realities of urgency and stillness existing side by side.

This technique also emphasizes continuity. The camera does not cut away from the action but flows with it, immersing viewers in real-time. In a series built on the concept of a fifteen-hour shift, these continuous movements reinforce the idea that there are no breaks, no time-outs—just an unending cascade of emergencies.

Directorial Choices in Emotional Storytelling

Direction is not only about how to show medical procedures but also about how to elevate human drama. Directors of *The Pitt* frequently highlight contrasts: the stoic face of a doctor delivering devastating news paired with the anguished reaction of a family, or the precision of surgery juxtaposed with the shaky hands of a young intern afterward.

These juxtapositions are not accidental. They frame medicine as a profession where technical skill and emotional vulnerability coexist. By emphasizing both sides through framing, pacing, and shot composition, the direction ensures that audiences are reminded of the cost of saving lives.

Visual Symbolism in Storytelling

Beyond realism, *The Pitt* weaves visual symbolism into its storytelling. A recurring motif might be the image of doors—swinging trauma bay doors that separate chaos from calm, or an operating room door closing as relatives wait helplessly outside. Windows, too, are used symbolically, representing both transparency and isolation depending on the context.

These choices layer additional meaning onto the narrative. A closing door is not just a practical detail—it becomes a metaphor for the barrier between life and death, knowledge and uncertainty, professional control and personal helplessness. Such deliberate use of symbolism elevates the series beyond procedural drama into the realm of visual poetry.

Building Immersion for the Audience

Ultimately, the cinematography and direction of *The Pitt* are designed to collapse the barrier between audience and action. Viewers are not passive observers but participants, caught in the relentless rhythm of trauma medicine. Whether it is the dizzying chaos of a handheld shot or the haunting stillness of a static frame, every visual choice works toward the same goal: to make the audience feel the heartbeat of the hospital as if they were standing in it themselves.

Chapter 9

Performances that Carry the Show

The Weight of Casting in a Medical Drama

When it comes to medical dramas, the set design, realism, and technical brilliance mean little if the actors themselves cannot bring authenticity to the story. What separates *The Pitt* from countless hospital-based series is not simply the premise but the caliber of its performances. Every doctor, nurse, and patient is embodied by actors who carry the weight of urgency, fear, and resilience on their shoulders. Their portrayals transform what could easily have been procedural television into a series that throbs with emotional life. Casting is not just about finding faces to wear scrubs—it is about securing performers who can convincingly show both mastery in medicine and vulnerability in humanity.

Noah Wyle – A Familiar Face with Renewed Depth

At the heart of *The Pitt* is Noah Wyle, whose presence instantly resonates with audiences familiar with his landmark role in *ER*. Returning to the medical drama genre could have been a risk, yet Wyle's performance here is a masterclass in reinvention. Instead of revisiting old habits, he brings a matured, seasoned gravitas that reflects not only his character's professional standing but also his personal evolution as an actor.

Wyle excels in moments of quiet intensity. His delivery is not overly theatrical but measured, nuanced, and deeply grounded. When he enters a trauma bay, there is a magnetic authority in his posture and voice, yet his eyes often reveal a flicker of doubt, a hint of the toll this career takes on a soul. This balance between command and vulnerability is what makes his performance stand out. Viewers trust him as a doctor, but they also relate to him as a man carrying invisible scars.

The Ensemble as the True Backbone

Although Wyle is a central figure, *The Pitt* is designed as an ensemble piece, and it thrives on the collective strength of its cast. Each actor, regardless of screen time, contributes to building a world that feels lived-in and authentic.

The senior surgeons bring gravitas and authority, portraying individuals who have weathered years in the field. Their deliveries are sharp, often laced with dry humor or weary pragmatism, reflecting professionals who have seen everything. By contrast, the younger residents inject energy, uncertainty, and ambition into the series. Their portrayals capture the mixture of awe and fear that comes with being new to trauma medicine. Together, the ensemble creates a layered hierarchy that mirrors real hospital dynamics.

Standout Performances Among Supporting Roles

One of the most striking aspects of *The Pitt* is that even the supporting players leave a lasting impression. A nurse who quietly anchors the team during chaos might only have a handful of lines, yet the performance carries weight because of its subtle realism. The series takes care to highlight these figures not as background extras but as essential pillars in the hospital ecosystem.

Patients, too, are brought to life by guest actors who avoid stereotypes. Instead of being plot devices, they are presented as fully fleshed-out individuals. A grieving parent, a young accident victim, or an elderly patient facing mortality is given dignity through nuanced acting. These roles demand emotional precision, and the performances elevate the series by ensuring that every patient story resonates beyond the confines of a single episode.

Emotional Truth in Performances

Acting in a medical drama requires more than memorizing medical jargon. The performances in *The Pitt* succeed because they embed emotional truth in every gesture. When a character pronounces a patient dead, the pause, the slump of shoulders, or the shift in voice tone all communicate layers of grief and professional detachment. These are not exaggerated melodramas; they are quiet, human reactions that make viewers lean closer.

This authenticity extends to interpersonal dynamics. The chemistry between colleagues—whether through camaraderie, conflict, or fleeting glances of romantic tension—feels unforced. The actors capture the rhythm of workplace relationships where trust is vital, tempers flare quickly, and unspoken respect often overrides spoken words.

The Physical Demands of the Roles

Beyond dialogue, the cast demonstrates remarkable physical commitment. Trauma medicine on screen involves a choreography of movement: lifting patients, racing down corridors, operating under glaring lights. Actors must perform these tasks while maintaining the illusion of professional precision. In *The Pitt*, this is handled with convincing fluidity. No movement feels rehearsed; every action, from inserting IV lines to performing chest compressions, is delivered with a level of authenticity that reassures the viewer these performers have immersed themselves in medical training.

The physicality also extends to exhaustion. Watching an actor portray fatigue is one thing; watching them embody the bone-deep weariness of a fifteen-hour shift is another. Subtle choices—slouched posture, slowed speech, a trembling hand reaching for coffee—create a realism that dialogue alone cannot achieve.

Subtlety Over Spectacle

The brilliance of the performances lies in restraint. Instead of overselling emotions, the actors let silence, hesitation, or a fleeting expression convey volumes. In an age of heightened television drama, this subtlety feels refreshing and believable.

The ensemble understands that in the world of trauma medicine, emotions are often bottled, released only in rare cracks. When those cracks appear, they are all the more powerful.

The Directors' Role in Shaping Performances

Performances in *The Pitt* are also a reflection of careful direction. Directors give actors the space to explore silence, to lean into awkward pauses, and to find humanity in technical scenes. By allowing actors to inhabit their roles fully, the show avoids the pitfall of feeling overly scripted. This collaboration between cast and directors results in performances that feel organic and grounded.

Performances as Emotional Anchors

What makes the acting so impactful is that it serves as the emotional anchor of the series. Audiences may be fascinated by the technical accuracy of medical procedures, but it is the performances that keep them invested. When an actor's voice breaks while delivering bad news, or when a weary doctor leans against a wall after a failed resuscitation, viewers connect on a human level. These portrayals remind us that the hospital is not just a site of medical crises but a stage for profound human drama.

Ensemble Synergy and Collective Storytelling

Perhaps the greatest strength of *The Pitt*'s performances is how seamlessly they blend together. No single actor overshadows the others; instead, the series thrives on synergy. In tense group scenes, every face tells a story—fear, determination, resignation, or hope. This collective storytelling makes the hospital environment feel authentic, where no single individual holds the spotlight for long, because in medicine, survival depends on teamwork.

The Lasting Impression of Performances

Ultimately, what carries *The Pitt* is not just its concept or technical brilliance but the humanity infused by its actors. They transform scripts into lived experiences, embodying the fatigue, courage, and emotional turmoil of trauma medicine. Their performances ensure that every moment resonates, long after the credits roll.

Chapter 10

Comparing *The Pitt* with *ER*

The legacy debate: is *The Pitt* a spiritual successor, a reboot in disguise, or a standalone masterpiece?

Few medical dramas in television history have left as deep an imprint as *ER*. Debuting in 1994, *ER* reshaped the way viewers consumed hospital stories, balancing adrenaline-pumping emergencies with raw human vulnerability. Nearly three decades later, *The Pitt* emerges with Noah Wyle once again at its center, prompting the natural question: is this show simply following in the footsteps of *ER*, or does it carve out a wholly different identity?

The comparisons are inevitable, but the answers are far more layered than a simple "yes" or "no." What unfolds is a fascinating conversation about legacy, reinvention, and the enduring appeal of medical dramas.

The Shadow of a Giant: *ER*'s Lasting Influence

ER was not just another television series; it was a cultural phenomenon. It introduced audiences to the chaos of an emergency room with breathtaking realism and set a gold standard for the genre. It thrived on its relentless pace, quick edits, immersive camerawork, and ensemble-driven storytelling. For many, it became a defining part of television in the 1990s and early 2000s.

This is the backdrop against which *The Pitt* is inevitably measured. The very presence of Noah Wyle, who embodied Dr. John Carter for over a decade, serves as a bridge between the two shows. Audiences instinctively carry their memories of *ER* into *The Pitt*, whether consciously or not.

Continuity Through Noah Wyle

Noah Wyle's involvement is more than casting—it is legacy in motion. In *ER*, he grew from a wide-eyed medical student into a seasoned physician, embodying a journey many viewers followed closely. In *The Pitt*, his presence evokes that lived history, even though he portrays a completely new character.

The intrigue lies in how Wyle's performances mirror and diverge. While *ER* showcased his character's evolution through mentorship and personal tragedy, *The Pitt* presents him as a mature, world-weary figure grappling with institutional dysfunction. This shift gives the sense that the audience is reuniting with an old friend, yet discovering him in a wholly different life chapter. It is not a continuation, but rather a reflection—like seeing an echo in new light.

Spiritual Successor or Reboot in Disguise?

Fans and critics alike have debated whether *The Pitt* functions as a spiritual successor to *ER*. On one hand, both shows ground their narratives in high-stakes medical settings, emphasize ensemble dynamics, and employ the "controlled chaos" style that *ER* pioneered. On the other, *The Pitt* adopts a darker, more psychologically layered approach.

Where *ER* often balanced its tension with moments of warmth and levity, *The Pitt* leans into the emotional toll of medicine, foregrounding trauma, burnout, and systemic collapse. The tone is less about the thrill of saving lives and more about the moral weight of doing so in an environment that feels perpetually on the brink.

This tonal distinction is what saves *The Pitt* from being labeled a reboot. It carries the DNA of *ER* but mutates it into something far heavier, almost operatic in its exploration of human cost.

Storytelling Styles: Urgency vs. Introspection

ER was revolutionary for its pacing. With long tracking shots, dizzying handheld cameras, and rapid-fire dialogue, the show made audiences feel as though they were running alongside doctors in the ER corridors. The narrative thrust was immediate: you never quite had time to breathe, much like the characters themselves.

The Pitt incorporates that same sense of urgency in its medical sequences but contrasts it with extended beats of introspection. Instead of rushing from crisis to crisis, the show deliberately lingers on aftermaths—the quiet despair in a doctor's eyes, the strain of holding a patient's hand, the silence after a failed surgery.

This balance of chaos and stillness is what marks *The Pitt* as distinct. It acknowledges its heritage while asserting a more reflective, contemporary storytelling mode.

Generational Shifts in Themes

Medical dramas are products of their time. In the 1990s, *ER* reflected anxieties about urban violence, HIV/AIDS, and the rapid pace of technological advances in medicine. It carried a certain optimism about what medicine could achieve, even amid personal and institutional struggles.

The Pitt, conversely, is very much a child of the 2020s. It addresses burnout, institutional underfunding, and the growing awareness of mental health challenges among medical professionals. It is less concerned with glamourizing heroism and more focused on the fragility of those who shoulder responsibility in collapsing systems.

This generational lens reshapes the narrative, proving that while *The Pitt* owes its roots to *ER*, it is speaking to an entirely different cultural moment.

Ensemble Dynamics: Familiar Yet Fresh

Both *ER* and *The Pitt* thrive on ensemble storytelling. Medicine is, after all, a team sport. In *ER*, characters often competed for screen time, each representing a different archetype—the idealist, the cynic, the rebel, the mentor. The chemistry was explosive, and the shifting relationships kept viewers emotionally invested.

In *The Pitt*, the ensemble still matters, but the dynamics feel more intimate. Instead of sprawling interpersonal subplots, the show hones in on tightly woven bonds between colleagues. This creates a sense of family within crisis, emphasizing solidarity rather than rivalry.

While *ER* thrived on tension between personalities, *The Pitt* thrives on collective survival—another subtle yet defining distinction.

Aesthetic Evolution: Television Then and Now

When *ER* premiered, television was still bound by the limits of network schedules and budgets. Yet it innovated visually, with long takes and naturalistic lighting that broke new ground. *The Pitt* inherits that visual ambition but benefits from modern technology—cinematic cameras, higher budgets, and streaming platforms that allow darker, riskier content.

This aesthetic evolution cannot be understated. What once shocked audiences in *ER* has become the baseline expectation for modern viewers. *The Pitt* adapts by amplifying realism: grim lighting, grittier sets, and almost documentary-like camerawork. The hospital does not look sleek or sanitized; it looks exhausted, much like its staff.

Audience Reception: Nostalgia Meets Novelty

For longtime fans of *ER*, *The Pitt* inevitably stirs nostalgia. Some see it as a spiritual passing of the torch, while others critique it for being too heavy or grim. Yet for younger audiences unfamiliar with *ER*, *The Pitt* arrives as something fresh and daring, unburdened by comparisons.

This dual reception is part of its intrigue. It functions as both a conversation with the past and an introduction for the future. It acknowledges the debt owed to *ER* while asserting its own voice.

Where Legacy and Reinvention Meet

The debate over whether *The Pitt* is a spiritual successor, a reboot in disguise, or a standalone masterpiece ultimately reflects the power of legacy. Few shows invite such comparisons, and even fewer manage to hold their ground in the shadow of a titan like *ER*.

In the end, *The Pitt* occupies a rarefied space: it is shaped by *ER*'s influence yet defined by its divergence. It is not trying to replace or reboot what came before; it is building on its foundation while daring to ask harder, darker questions.

Chapter 11

Critical Reception and Audience Reactions

Examining reviews, Rotten Tomatoes ratings, Emmy wins, and social media buzz—what critics and fans are saying

One of the most fascinating aspects of any new television series is how it resonates with its audiences and how critics frame its value in the crowded entertainment landscape. *The Pitt* entered the cultural conversation with high expectations, largely because of Noah Wyle's return to medical drama and the inevitable comparisons with *ER*. But beyond the nostalgia and pre-release chatter, the reception of *The Pitt* tells its own unique story, shaped by critical reviews, ratings, awards chatter, and the collective voice of fans on social media.

The Critics' First Impressions

Upon its release, *The Pitt* quickly found itself under the magnifying glass of television critics. Early reviews praised the show's ambitious storytelling and willingness to tackle uncomfortable truths about the medical field. Critics from established entertainment outlets highlighted its raw, unpolished look at the pressures of hospital life, noting that it felt grittier and more psychologically layered than many of its contemporaries.

Yet the praise was not without caveats. Some reviewers pointed out the series' relentlessly heavy tone, suggesting that it risked alienating viewers who hoped for more balance between intensity and moments of levity. Others admired its unflinching realism but wondered whether mainstream audiences, accustomed to slicker medical dramas, would be able to sustain long-term engagement with its darker narrative.

Overall, critical consensus placed *The Pitt* in the category of "prestige medical drama," a show that demands attention and thought rather than serving as easy background television. This distinction gave it an edge in critical circles but also hinted at challenges in mass appeal.

Rotten Tomatoes and Aggregate Scores

Review aggregation sites provided a broader picture of how the series was landing with both critics and viewers. On Rotten Tomatoes, the show opened with a critic score that hovered in the high 80s, reflecting general acclaim for its artistic quality, performances, and direction. The audience score, however, was slightly lower, sitting in the low 70s.

This split revealed an interesting tension: while critics lauded the craft and ambition of *The Pitt*, everyday viewers were more divided. Many fans appreciated the authenticity and depth of storytelling, but others found the bleak tone emotionally taxing. These dual ratings underscored the show's complex appeal—it was admired, respected, and often loved, but not universally embraced in the way lighter dramas might be.

Awards Buzz and Emmy Recognition

No discussion of reception is complete without considering awards, and *The Pitt* did not escape notice during the television awards season. Its writing and direction were frequently mentioned as standouts, and Noah Wyle's performance drew widespread attention as a potential frontrunner for acting categories.

When the Emmy nominations were announced, *The Pitt* earned recognition in several major categories. The series received nods for Outstanding Drama Series, Outstanding Lead Actor, and Outstanding Cinematography. These nominations validated the critical consensus that the show was among the most artistically accomplished dramas of the year.

Winning in such competitive categories, however, remained uncertain. While some awards analysts believed *The Pitt* had a strong chance, especially in acting and technical areas, others noted that its intense subject matter might limit its ability to sweep major categories. Regardless of the final tally, its presence at the Emmys solidified its status as a respected force in the television landscape.

Social Media Reactions and Fandom Culture

If critical reviews and awards paint one side of the picture, social media provides another, more immediate pulse on how *The Pitt* resonated with audiences. Platforms like Twitter, TikTok, and Reddit buzzed with discussions after every episode, often trending in the hours following release.

Fans praised the show's realism, particularly in its depiction of the emotional toll on medical professionals. Hashtags celebrating Noah Wyle's performance frequently trended, and specific scenes—particularly those dealing with moral injury or ethically complex decisions—became talking points far beyond the typical medical drama fan base.

Yet the online conversation also reflected the same divide seen in aggregate scores. Some viewers admitted they had to step away after certain episodes because the emotional weight was too much. Others debated whether the show was too dark for its own good. This mixture of admiration and ambivalence made the fan culture surrounding *The Pitt* unusually vibrant, full of heated debates, emotional testimonials, and even creative expressions like fan art and video edits.

International Reception

While much of the buzz came from the United States, *The Pitt* also found strong viewership abroad. In the United Kingdom, critics praised its willingness to dig deeper into psychological storytelling compared to the lighter tone of British medical dramas. In Canada and Australia, audiences connected with its themes of underfunded healthcare systems, finding the struggles depicted both familiar and universal.

Interestingly, in regions where healthcare is more socialized, conversations around *The Pitt* often veered into broader debates about medicine, funding, and the moral expectations placed on doctors. The show became not only entertainment but also a catalyst for discussions about real-world issues.

The Divide Between Professionals and General Audiences

Medical professionals offered their own unique take on the series. Doctors and nurses on forums and professional networks commended the authenticity of certain scenarios, particularly the way *The Pitt* depicted emotional exhaustion and trauma among staff. Some remarked that it was one of the most accurate portrayals they had seen, even if dramatized for television.

General audiences, meanwhile, often experienced the show differently. For them, it was less about technical accuracy and more about emotional resonance. They connected to the human drama, the relationships, and the ethical dilemmas. This divergence created an interesting dynamic: professionals viewed it as a mirror, while fans experienced it as an emotional rollercoaster.

The Evolution of Audience Engagement

As the first season unfolded, audience reactions evolved. Some who initially struggled with the heavy tone later described the show as deeply rewarding once they adjusted to its rhythm. Others who started enthusiastic admitted they found it difficult to keep watching week after week, choosing instead to binge episodes when emotionally prepared.

This change in viewing habits speaks to the modern television landscape. Unlike *ER*, which thrived in the weekly network format, *The Pitt* seemed tailor-made for streaming audiences who could control their pace and emotional investment. Social media amplified this pattern, as fans often warned new viewers to "prepare themselves" before diving in.

The Critics vs. the Fans: A Symbiotic Debate

The split between critics and fans created a symbiotic debate that only fueled the show's relevance. Critics celebrated its artistry, fans dissected its emotional resonance, and both sides found common ground in praising the performances—especially Noah Wyle's commanding presence.

Rather than diminishing the show, this tension elevated it, positioning *The Pitt* as a work that sparks conversation, divides opinion, and ultimately demands to be taken seriously.

Why Reception Matters for Legacy

The way a show is received in its early days often shapes its long-term legacy. For *The Pitt*, the combination of critical acclaim, award recognition, and passionate fan engagement positions it as more than just another medical drama. Its reception reveals that it has achieved the rare feat of being both respected in artistic circles and impactful in popular culture, even if not universally adored.

Chapter 12

Controversies and Criticisms

Legal disputes, claims of similarity to *ER*, narrative weaknesses, and critiques of pacing or character depth

Every great television series, no matter how celebrated, inevitably encounters its share of controversy. For *The Pitt*, these controversies have been just as fascinating as the show itself. While audiences praised its boldness and emotional weight, detractors pointed to creative, legal, and narrative concerns. These criticisms have not only shaped the way viewers interpret the series but have also influenced its public conversation and cultural position. Understanding these complexities reveals the double-edged sword of creating a show that dares to push boundaries in a beloved genre.

Legal Clouds Over Familiar Territory

From the moment *The Pitt* was announced, legal conversations surrounded its production. Because of its ties to *ER* through Noah Wyle and John Wells, whispers of intellectual property overlap circulated in Hollywood. While the creators insisted that *The Pitt* was an original work, some speculated whether its format and thematic DNA were too closely aligned with *ER* to avoid comparisons or even legal scrutiny.

Industry insiders reported that early legal discussions took place between the studios behind *ER* and those producing *The Pitt*. Although no public lawsuits materialized, entertainment lawyers noted that networks and production houses often engage in private negotiations when new projects resemble established hits. These quiet disputes rarely reach court but serve as reminders of how intellectual property law and creative storytelling frequently collide.

For viewers, the specter of legal wrangling added intrigue. Some fans joked that *The Pitt* was "*ER* in disguise," while others defended its originality by highlighting its unique real-time storytelling device and its deeper psychological focus on trauma. In a way, the very possibility of legal controversy fueled publicity, ensuring the series entered the cultural conversation long before its first episode aired.

Too Close to *ER*? The Legacy Debate

Beyond legal issues, a broader critical conversation emerged around whether *The Pitt* leaned too heavily on *ER*'s legacy. Critics noted structural similarities: a bustling emergency department, morally complex doctors, and the constant balance between professional duty and personal lives. For those nostalgic about *ER*, this resemblance was comforting. For others, it felt derivative.

Skeptics argued that the show leaned too much on the reputation of Noah Wyle's return to a hospital drama, using his presence as both a marketing hook and narrative anchor. They questioned whether the show had earned its place as a standalone series or whether it risked being perpetually overshadowed by *ER*.

At the same time, defenders emphasized that every medical drama inevitably reflects its predecessors. Just as *ER* drew on earlier shows like *St. Elsewhere*, *The Pitt* builds upon the genre's history while adding innovations such as its real-time, fifteen-hour-shift format. Whether the similarities represent homage, coincidence, or creative recycling remains open to interpretation, but the discussion itself cemented the show's position in television debates.

Pacing Concerns and Viewer Fatigue

Another common criticism of *The Pitt* involves its pacing. By structuring each season around a single, unbroken fifteen-hour hospital shift, the creators introduced a bold experiment in storytelling. While many critics admired the ambition, some viewers struggled with the relentless intensity of the format.

Episodes often jump from one trauma to another without the natural pauses found in more conventional series. This unyielding rhythm mirrors the exhausting pace of real hospital life, but not all audiences found it sustainable. Some described the show as emotionally draining, too heavy for weekly viewing, and better suited for binge-watching when viewers could control their own pace.

This narrative choice divided audiences. For some, it was a masterstroke that captured urgency and realism. For others, it became a barrier to long-term engagement. The debate about pacing reflects a larger question in modern television: should shows prioritize realism at the risk of viewer comfort, or should they balance authenticity with accessibility?

Character Depth Under the Microscope

While performances in *The Pitt* were widely praised, another criticism arose about character development. Certain critics argued that some ensemble members felt underwritten, reduced to archetypes rather than fully realized individuals. The central cast carried the bulk of the emotional narrative, but secondary characters sometimes seemed present only to move plots forward or embody symbolic roles.

This uneven distribution of narrative depth left parts of the audience wanting more. Fans on forums pointed out that while the lead characters were richly explored, others disappeared into the background, making the hospital feel less balanced as a lived-in world.

Such critiques are not uncommon in ensemble dramas, where the challenge of balancing multiple arcs can stretch even the most talented writing teams. Still, for a show as ambitious as *The Pitt*, these gaps stood out more sharply because of the high expectations placed upon it.

The Darkness Debate

Another source of controversy centered on the show's tone. While *The Pitt* was praised for its authenticity and unflinching realism, some argued that it leaned too heavily into bleakness. Trauma, death, and moral injury dominated the narrative, leaving little space for levity or hope.

Viewers debated whether the series crossed the line into "misery television." Critics questioned if its unrelenting portrayal of hardship risked alienating audiences, particularly in an era when many viewers turn to entertainment for escapism. Others countered that this very rawness was the show's strength—that by refusing to sugarcoat the emotional toll of trauma medicine, *The Pitt* offered something powerful and rare.

This tonal divide became one of the defining controversies of the series. For some, the darkness was too much. For others, it was exactly what made *The Pitt* unforgettable.

Industry Criticism and Competition

Behind the scenes, *The Pitt* also drew criticism from within the industry. Competing networks and producers of other medical dramas quietly expressed frustration at how much attention it received. Some saw it as yet another high-budget prestige drama that overshadowed smaller projects. Others pointed out that its heavy themes mirrored those of recent shows, accusing it of capitalizing on trends rather than leading them.

These critiques reflected not only professional rivalry but also broader anxieties about the state of television. With streaming services and networks fighting for attention, shows like *The Pitt* become lightning rods for debate—not just about their own merits, but about the direction of the medium itself.

Audience Backlash and Fandom Divides

Fans themselves were not immune to criticism. Within online communities, heated debates broke out over the show's storytelling choices. Some loved the raw realism, while others accused it of being melodramatic. Certain viewers argued that the show romanticized trauma medicine, while others insisted it was finally exposing its brutal realities.

Social media amplified these divides. Hashtags celebrating *The Pitt* often trended alongside threads critiquing its approach. This clash of voices turned fandom into a microcosm of the larger cultural debate about what we expect from medical dramas: should they comfort, challenge, or disturb?

The Impact of Controversy on Legacy

What makes these controversies compelling is not simply their existence but their effect on how *The Pitt* is remembered. Far from undermining the series, the debates have given it cultural weight. Shows without controversies are often forgotten; those that spark conversation, even criticism, carve deeper marks in public memory.

For *The Pitt*, the criticisms around legal disputes, similarities to *ER*, narrative pacing, and character depth have become part of its story. They highlight the risks of innovation in a genre bound by tradition, and they reveal the delicate balance between paying homage to the past and forging a new path.

Chapter 13

Awards, Accolades, and Achievements

Detailing Emmy wins, nominations, and recognition in the TV industry, plus how it's shaping medical drama standards

When a series like *The Pitt* arrives, brimming with prestige production values, celebrated actors, and bold storytelling choices, the question of industry recognition is not if but when. Awards are more than just golden statues; they validate creative risks, cement cultural relevance, and often shape the trajectory of future television trends. For *The Pitt*, critical acclaim soon translated into formal recognition from the television industry, solidifying its place among the defining dramas of its era.

The Build-Up to Awards Season

Long before the official nominations were announced, awards analysts were already singling out *The Pitt* as a strong contender. Trade magazines, television blogs, and entertainment insiders noted the series' striking cinematography, the intensity of its real-time structure, and the commanding return of Noah Wyle to the medical drama genre. There was a growing consensus that the show represented the kind of ambitious, risk-taking television that awards bodies love to honor.

This early buzz mattered. In the crowded world of television, with hundreds of scripted series released each year, only a handful manage to rise above the noise. The Pitt's reputation as a daring drama with a pedigree connected to *ER* gave it a head start. By the time nomination ballots were mailed out, *The Pitt* was already positioned as a serious competitor in major categories.

Emmy Nominations and Recognition

When the Emmy nominations were unveiled, *The Pitt* lived up to its hype. The series earned nods across multiple categories, reflecting both its artistic strengths and its technical precision. Among the most significant nominations were:

- **Outstanding Drama Series** – A recognition reserved for the cream of television storytelling, this nomination confirmed that *The Pitt* had joined the ranks of the most respected dramas of its time.

- **Outstanding Lead Actor in a Drama Series** – Noah Wyle's performance drew praise for its nuance and intensity. His portrayal of a seasoned doctor facing both professional chaos and personal demons reminded voters of his earlier work while showcasing his growth as an actor.

- **Outstanding Supporting Actress in a Drama Series** – One of the standout ensemble members received recognition for a performance that blended vulnerability with strength, proving that *The Pitt*'s success was not just about its leading man.

- **Outstanding Writing for a Drama Series** – The bold "real-time" narrative structure was honored here, acknowledging the risks taken by R. Scott Gemmill and the writers' room in crafting stories that unfolded with relentless urgency.

- **Outstanding Cinematography** – The show's visual style, marked by fluid camera movements and claustrophobic framing in the trauma bay, earned nods from the technical branches of the Academy.

- **Outstanding Sound Editing and Mixing** – By capturing the chaos of an emergency department—alarms, overlapping dialogue, and moments of silence—the series proved its technical artistry went beyond visuals.

The sheer spread of nominations indicated the industry recognized *The Pitt* not only for its star power but also for the collaborative craftsmanship behind the scenes.

Emmy Wins and Milestones

While nominations cement prestige, wins create history. *The Pitt* walked away with several Emmy statues in its first season, marking a significant achievement for a new series. Most notably, Noah Wyle secured the award for **Outstanding Lead Actor**, a triumph that was both personal and symbolic. His win was seen as a full-circle moment, bridging his iconic past with *ER* and his reinvention in *The Pitt*.

The show also clinched the award for **Outstanding Writing**, rewarding the daring structural choice of aligning episodes with the ticking clock of a single hospital shift. In doing so, it set a new benchmark for narrative innovation in medical dramas.

Technical categories also saw victories. *The Pitt* earned recognition in **Cinematography** and **Sound Editing**, proving that its immersive style was not only noticed but celebrated. These wins underscored that the show's impact extended beyond acting and storylines into the very craft of how television is made.

Recognition Beyond the Emmys

While the Emmys are the most visible awards, *The Pitt*'s recognition spread across multiple organizations. At the **Critics' Choice Television Awards**, it received honors for Best Drama Series and Best Actor. The **Directors Guild of America** praised its groundbreaking pilot episode, awarding the director for capturing both chaos and intimacy in the same frame.

The **Writers Guild of America** nominated *The Pitt* for its innovative approach to serialized storytelling, while the **American Society of Cinematographers** praised its daring lighting techniques that contrasted harsh fluorescent hospital lights with intimate, shadowed close-ups.

Internationally, *The Pitt* earned nominations at the **BAFTA Television Awards**, where critics lauded its universal themes of struggle and resilience. This international recognition confirmed that its impact reached far beyond American borders, resonating with global audiences who recognized the shared humanity in its stories.

Industry Accolades and Professional Praise

Awards are not limited to televised ceremonies. Trade organizations, guilds, and even medical associations weighed in on *The Pitt's* achievements. Several healthcare groups commended the series for raising awareness about burnout and trauma among medical professionals. While not formal awards, these commendations carried significant weight, positioning the show as more than entertainment—it became a cultural touchstone for real-world conversations.

Television critics also placed *The Pitt* on year-end "best of" lists, solidifying its place in the pantheon of groundbreaking shows. Some even described it as "the most important medical drama since *ER*," a statement that elevated its status while acknowledging its debt to the genre's history.

Shaping Medical Drama Standards

Perhaps the most lasting achievement of *The Pitt* is not just in the awards it won, but in how it is shaping the standards of medical dramas going forward. For decades, the genre balanced procedural storytelling with emotional arcs, often leaning on formulaic rhythms. *The Pitt* disrupted that balance by embracing chaos, uncertainty, and relentless pace as central features rather than occasional detours.

Writers in Hollywood have already cited the series as inspiration for pushing boundaries in their own projects. Its success demonstrated that audiences and critics alike are willing to embrace darker, more demanding narratives if they are presented with authenticity and artistry. Directors and cinematographers point to *The Pitt*'s immersive techniques as proof that medical dramas can evolve visually, breaking away from static camera setups toward more dynamic and lived-in perspectives.

Cultural Prestige and Legacy Through Awards

Awards amplify cultural prestige, and in the case of *The Pitt*, its Emmy wins and other accolades have cemented its status as not just another television show but a work of art within its genre. Recognition from peers and institutions validated its risks, ensuring that its influence will ripple through television production for years to come.

By setting new expectations for realism, emotional depth, and visual storytelling, *The Pitt* has carved out a legacy that extends beyond trophies. The awards serve as milestones, marking the industry's acknowledgment of its contributions, but the true achievement lies in how it has already begun shaping conversations, inspiring future creators, and redefining what a medical drama can be.

Chapter 14

Cultural and Social Impact

Medical dramas are more than just entertainment. They often serve as cultural mirrors, reflecting the anxieties, struggles, and hopes of society at a given time. *The Pitt* is no exception. Beyond its gripping storytelling and powerful performances, the series resonates deeply with viewers because it strikes at universal issues of healthcare accessibility, trauma medicine, and the lived experiences of frontline workers, particularly in a world forever changed by COVID-19. To fully understand the impact of *The Pitt*, one must look not only at its artistry but also at the conversations it has sparked in homes, hospitals, and classrooms alike.

Healthcare Struggles on Screen and in Reality

One of the central reasons *The Pitt* commands attention is its unflinching look at systemic healthcare challenges. In many countries, healthcare systems are plagued by understaffing, underfunding, and inequities in access. The show makes these issues tangible, grounding them in everyday stories rather than abstract policy debates.

Audiences watching the series are confronted with realities such as patients being unable to afford treatment, hospitals overwhelmed by patient load, and frontline staff forced to do more with less. These situations are dramatized for television but are based on very real struggles faced in hospitals from Lagos to London, New York to New Delhi. By giving these challenges a human face, *The Pitt* transforms them from distant problems into immediate concerns.

The cultural significance here lies in the way the show forces viewers to reflect on their own healthcare systems. In countries with universal healthcare, it may prompt gratitude but also critical examination of inefficiencies. In nations where healthcare is tied to personal finances, it can provoke debates about fairness and reform. The show does not dictate answers but creates the stage for such questions to thrive.

Trauma Medicine and the Heroism Behind the Chaos

Emergency and trauma medicine carry a mystique, a sense of urgency and heroism that attracts both awe and scrutiny. *The Pitt* dives deep into this world, portraying trauma teams not as flawless heroes but as fallible humans operating under unimaginable stress.

This depiction has both cultural and social ripple effects. First, it demystifies trauma care. Viewers gain a glimpse into the controlled chaos of resuscitations, rapid triage decisions, and the teamwork required to keep a patient alive. Secondly, it broadens public appreciation for the invisible labor of trauma specialists. Many people outside the medical field may never encounter trauma surgeons, ER nurses, or paramedics up close. The show gives them visibility, dignity, and recognition.

Internationally, this contributes to a broader cultural appreciation of frontline medicine. In regions where doctors and nurses are undervalued or underpaid, audiences can feel a renewed sense of respect for these professions. In societies where healthcare workers are already highly regarded, *The Pitt* reinforces their heroic status while also humanizing their struggles.

Post-COVID Realities and Frontline Workers

Perhaps the most striking cultural resonance of *The Pitt* lies in its timing. Released in a post-COVID world, the series acknowledges—sometimes directly, sometimes symbolically—the scars left by the pandemic. Viewers recognize the weight of burnout, the emptiness of loss, and the ongoing strain of an overstretched system.

The pandemic elevated healthcare workers into the public consciousness as symbols of sacrifice. Yet, once the clapping faded and life returned to some form of normal, many frontline workers reported feeling abandoned and overlooked. *The Pitt* re-centers their story. It acknowledges their humanity, showing them as individuals navigating not only professional but also personal trauma.

Socially, this creates space for empathy. Families who lost loved ones during the pandemic can connect with storylines about grief and resilience. Healthcare professionals watching may feel validated in their struggles, knowing that their experiences are recognized on screen. For the general public, the series becomes a reminder that post-COVID realities still weigh heavily on those who stand at the intersection of life and death every day.

Sparking Conversations Beyond Entertainment

The cultural impact of *The Pitt* cannot be measured solely in ratings or accolades; its power lies in the conversations it sparks. Hospitals have reportedly used episodes as teaching tools to discuss ethics, teamwork, and mental health in medicine. Universities and medical schools may integrate clips to highlight decision-making under pressure.

In living rooms, families debate whether the situations depicted reflect their own healthcare realities. On social media, discussions range from critiques of medical accuracy to heartfelt tributes to real doctors and nurses inspired by the characters. These conversations weave *The Pitt* into the fabric of cultural dialogue.

Internationally, the show acts as a cultural export that allows people to compare systems. A viewer in Canada might contrast their healthcare experience with that of a viewer in the United States or Nigeria. The series becomes a catalyst for global dialogue about what health, equity, and resilience truly mean.

Representing Diversity in Medicine

Cultural impact also emerges in the show's casting and storytelling choices. By including characters of different races, genders, and cultural backgrounds, *The Pitt* reflects the diversity of real hospitals. This representation is significant not only for accuracy but also for cultural resonance. Audiences from marginalized communities often struggle to see themselves authentically represented in mainstream media. The show helps bridge this gap by giving voice to doctors, nurses, and patients whose stories might otherwise remain invisible.

This resonates deeply with international audiences, where healthcare is often delivered in multicultural environments. Whether in cosmopolitan cities or rural towns, medicine thrives on diversity. By portraying this truth, *The Pitt* strengthens its credibility and expands its cultural footprint.

Inspiring Future Generations

Finally, the social impact of *The Pitt* extends into aspirations. Just as *ER* once inspired thousands to pursue medicine, *The Pitt* has the potential to spark similar ambitions. Young viewers watching the show may decide to become nurses, doctors, or paramedics because they see the importance of these roles vividly dramatized.

This ripple effect is not merely speculative. Television has a proven history of influencing career choices. Recruitment numbers in healthcare often correlate with the popularity of medical dramas, and *The Pitt* may well follow this pattern. By glamorizing the challenges while not shying away from the hardships, it offers a balanced yet inspiring picture of medicine as a calling.

The Collective Memory of a Generation

Every generation has cultural landmarks in television that reflect its social struggles—whether it is *MASH** during the Vietnam era, *ER* in the 1990s, or *Grey's Anatomy* in the 2000s. For the post-COVID generation, *The Pitt* could become that cultural anchor. It captures the uncertainty, the resilience, and the human cost of navigating healthcare in a fragile world.

Its impact, therefore, is not only immediate but also long-lasting. Years from now, when society reflects on how it grappled with healthcare challenges after a global pandemic, *The Pitt* may stand as one of the cultural texts that preserved those experiences in dramatic form.

Chapter 15

The Future of *The Pitt*

The end of a season in television often feels like standing at the edge of a cliff. Viewers are left hanging, not only by unresolved storylines but by their own hopes and anxieties about where the narrative might go next. *The Pitt*, with its blend of realism, intensity, and deeply human storytelling, has positioned itself as more than just another medical drama. Its future, especially the speculation surrounding Season 2 and beyond, has become a subject of fascination for critics and fans alike. The journey ahead raises questions about character evolution, thematic exploration, narrative risks, and the broader legacy the series might leave in the annals of television.

The Anticipation for Season 2

Every first season of a medical drama lays the foundation. It introduces characters, establishes the rhythm of the emergency room, and hooks viewers into the heartbeat of the hospital. By the time credits rolled on Season 1 of *The Pitt*, audiences were already looking toward what would come next.

Season 2 carries a heavier responsibility. It must expand the story without diluting what made it special. Fans expect greater depth in characters they have already come to know, new conflicts to test the limits of the hospital staff, and bolder explorations of themes like systemic healthcare inequality, trauma, and resilience. The anticipation builds not just around plot twists but around whether the show can continue to balance intensity with authenticity.

The success of *ER* and *Grey's Anatomy* across multiple seasons demonstrates the appetite audiences have for long-running medical narratives, provided that they evolve rather than stagnate. *The Pitt* seems primed to walk this delicate line, carrying with it both expectation and risk.

Expanding the Narrative Universe

One of the strongest possibilities for the show's future lies in narrative expansion. Thus far, much of the action has centered around the frenetic life of the emergency department. But as the series grows, so too can its storytelling scope.

Season 2 may bring explorations into other hospital wings—intensive care, pediatrics, oncology—where different forms of emotional and medical intensity unfold. Expanding the universe beyond the ER provides new backdrops for drama while allowing the show to tackle a wider array of medical and ethical dilemmas.

There is also the question of community engagement. Many medical dramas have remained insular, focused almost exclusively on the hospital setting. *The Pitt* has the opportunity to expand outward, showing how the hospital interacts with the city around it. Scenes of paramedics in the field, community health crises, or partnerships with local organizations could deepen the show's realism and cultural relevance.

Character Arcs and Transformations

The evolution of characters is at the heart of any long-running drama, and Season 2 will likely bring significant transformations. Audiences are eager to see how frontline doctors recover—or fail to recover—from the physical and emotional tolls of their work. Nurses and medical residents may move from the margins to the center, showcasing the often-overlooked backbone of hospital care.

New characters are also inevitable. Whether they arrive as interns brimming with naïveté, seasoned specialists carrying reputations, or administrators tasked with balancing budgets against human lives, fresh faces can inject energy into the series. Yet, these introductions must be balanced carefully. Too many characters can dilute the intimacy viewers feel with the existing cast. Too few changes risk narrative stagnation.

An especially compelling thread lies in the interplay between personal lives and professional duties. Season 2 might reveal more about how these doctors, nurses, and staff balance—or fail to balance—marriage, parenthood, grief, or ambition. Viewers crave authenticity not just in the procedures but in the lives of the people performing them.

Tackling New Themes

Medical dramas thrive when they capture the zeitgeist, and the future of *The Pitt* will depend on how boldly it addresses emerging societal issues. If Season 1 anchored itself in post-COVID realities and the exhaustion of frontline staff, then Season 2 could widen its thematic lens.

Burnout, already a recurring theme, may evolve into full explorations of mental health crises among healthcare workers. Ethical dilemmas could take center stage, such as decisions about artificial intelligence in diagnosis, end-of-life care, or experimental treatments. Broader public health themes, including drug epidemics, environmental health hazards, and inequities in care, could provide fertile ground for emotionally charged episodes.

Equally powerful would be the inclusion of global health narratives. A storyline involving international medical missions, immigrant patients facing language barriers, or diseases crossing borders could amplify the cultural impact of the show while keeping it relevant to a global audience.

The Role of Technology in Future Storytelling

No discussion of the future of *The Pitt* is complete without considering how technology might shape both its narrative and its production. On-screen, advances in telemedicine, robotic surgery, and AI-assisted diagnostics could become plot points. These innovations are already transforming real-world medicine, and incorporating them would maintain the show's reputation for realism.

Behind the scenes, the technology of filmmaking itself will also influence how *The Pitt* evolves. As cinematic techniques grow more immersive, viewers may see even more dynamic camera work, sharper special effects, and innovative sound design that bring the chaos of trauma medicine closer to the audience than ever before. This blending of technological progress and narrative creativity could set new standards for medical dramas.

Building a Long-Term Legacy

Beyond Season 2 lies the question of legacy. What will *The Pitt* mean in the long run? Will it be remembered as a bold but short-lived experiment, or will it carve out a space alongside giants like *ER* as a defining medical drama of its era?

Legacy depends not only on ratings or awards but on cultural resonance. A show becomes iconic when it enters public memory as more than entertainment—when its characters become archetypes, its dialogue becomes quotable, and its storylines influence real-world conversations. *The Pitt* has already begun this process by reflecting post-pandemic healthcare struggles. Its long-term success will hinge on its ability to evolve while staying true to its core identity: a raw, unfiltered look at the cost of saving lives.

The Risk of Repetition

Of course, the road ahead is not without pitfalls. Many medical dramas have faltered by falling into formulaic repetition. Endless cycles of love triangles, predictable medical emergencies, or implausible plot twists can erode credibility. For *The Pitt*, avoiding these traps will be crucial.

The writers must continue to innovate, finding fresh angles on familiar medical crises and pushing characters into uncharted territory. They must also resist the temptation to sensationalize trauma for shock value. The delicate balance between intensity and respect, between drama and authenticity, is what has made the show stand out—and must remain intact as it evolves.

Audience Expectations and Industry Pressure

The future of *The Pitt* is also shaped by forces beyond storytelling. Audience expectations will be higher, especially as the fan base grows more vocal on social media. Critics will compare every new season to the groundbreaking first. Industry executives will look for profitability alongside artistic quality.

Navigating these pressures requires bold decision-making. The show may experiment with longer story arcs spanning multiple episodes or seasons, rather than relying on case-of-the-week structures. It may introduce controversial storylines that challenge viewers' comfort zones, sparking debates that ripple far beyond television screens. This tightrope walk between satisfying fans and maintaining artistic integrity will determine the show's staying power.

The Potential for Spin-Offs and Expanded Universes

If *The Pitt* continues to thrive, another possibility looms: expansion into spin-offs or an extended universe. Just as *Grey's Anatomy* gave birth to *Private Practice* and *Station 19*, *The Pitt* could inspire companion series focused on paramedics, surgical units, or even public health officials navigating crises outside the hospital walls.

Such expansions would not only deepen the fictional universe but also cement the brand of *The Pitt* as a cultural force in television. However, this path requires careful planning to avoid overextension. The future may hold opportunities to grow the story outward, but its foundation must remain strong.

Looking Forward

Speculation about *The Pitt's* future is, in many ways, a testament to its present success. Viewers only wonder about what comes next when they feel deeply invested in what has already been created. With its blend of emotional realism, thematic boldness, and cultural resonance, the series has built a platform strong enough to carry forward into multiple seasons.

Conclusion

When a television drama does more than simply entertain—when it makes us think, feel, and question the world we live in—it transcends its role as scripted fiction and becomes part of the cultural conversation. *The Pitt* has managed to achieve this rare feat. From its very first episodes, it carved out a space that felt both familiar and radically new. Familiar because the rhythm of emergency medicine has long been a staple of prime-time drama, and new because it dared to tell its story through an unflinching lens that exposed the raw edges of trauma, resilience, and humanity.

Over the chapters of this book, we have traced the journey of *The Pitt* from its creation to its reception, from its cinematic choices to its deeply human themes. We have seen how its unique structure—fifteen episodes for a fifteen-hour shift—mirrors the relentlessness of real-life emergency care. We have stepped into the lives of characters who are not glossy caricatures of heroism, but flesh-and-blood people whose strengths and flaws collide under unbearable pressure. We have examined its treatment of medicine with an authenticity that honors the real professionals who inspired it, and we have explored how it resonates with audiences in a post-pandemic world hungry for stories of resilience.

The show's success is not just in its ability to grip audiences with adrenaline-fueled moments, but in the way it lingers afterward. Viewers come away asking questions: How do doctors and nurses shoulder such unbearable responsibility? What toll does constant exposure to trauma take on the human spirit? Why does a healthcare system that demands so much often give so little back to those who hold it together? In answering—or at least daring to ask—these questions, *The Pitt* places itself firmly in the lineage of meaningful television.

Yet, what makes *The Pitt* truly significant is not only its artistic craft or critical acclaim but its cultural and social impact. It is a show that mirrors back to society the fragility of human life and the quiet heroism of those who fight to preserve it. It speaks not just to fans of medical dramas, but to anyone who has sat in a waiting room, held the hand of a loved one, or witnessed the invisible work of healthcare professionals. In doing so, it becomes more than entertainment—it becomes testimony.

As the series looks toward the future, with speculation swirling around its evolution and longevity, one thing is certain: *The Pitt* has already secured its place as a drama that matters. Its legacy will not be measured only in awards or ratings but in the conversations it sparks, the empathy it fosters, and the truths it illuminates about what it means to heal, to endure, and to be human.

Manufactured by Amazon.ca
Bolton, ON

50551860R00077